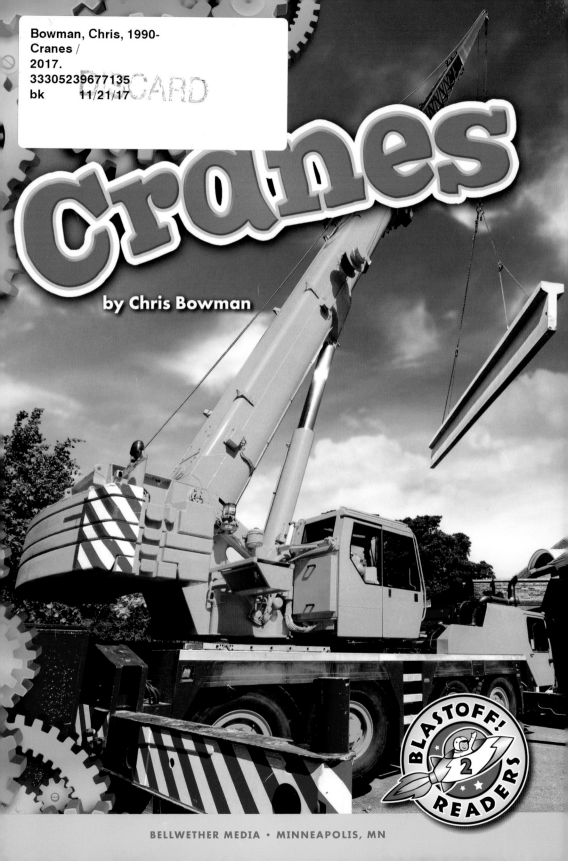

Cranes

by Chris Bowman

BELLWETHER MEDIA • MINNEAPOLIS, MN

BLASTOFF!
2
READERS

Note to Librarians, Teachers, and Parents:

Blastoff! Readers are carefully developed by literacy experts and combine standards-based content with developmentally appropriate text.

Level 1 provides the most support through repetition of high-frequency words, light text, predictable sentence patterns, and strong visual support.

Level 2 offers early readers a bit more challenge through varied simple sentences, increased text load, and less repetition of high-frequency words.

Level 3 advances early-fluent readers toward fluency through increased text and concept load, less reliance on visuals, longer sentences, and more literary language.

Level 4 builds reading stamina by providing more text per page, increased use of punctuation, greater variation in sentence patterns, and increasingly challenging vocabulary.

Level 5 encourages children to move from "learning to read" to "reading to learn" by providing even more text, varied writing styles, and less familiar topics.

Whichever book is right for your reader, Blastoff! Readers are the perfect books to build confidence and encourage a love of reading that will last a lifetime!

This edition first published in 2017 by Bellwether Media, Inc.

No part of this publication may be reproduced in whole or in part without written permission of the publisher. For information regarding permission, write to Bellwether Media, Inc., Attention: Permissions Department, 5357 Penn Avenue South, Minneapolis, MN 55419.

Library of Congress Cataloging-in-Publication Data

Names: Bowman, Chris, 1990- author.
Title: Cranes / by Chris Bowman.
Description: Minneapolis, MN : Bellwether Media, Inc., 2017. | Series: Blastoff! Readers. Mighty Machines in Action |
    Audience: Ages 5-8. | Audience: K to grade 3. | Includes bibliographical references and index.
Identifiers: LCCN 2016033332 (print) | LCCN 2016035421 (ebook) | ISBN 9781626176027
    (hardcover : alk. paper) | ISBN 9781681033327 (ebook)
Subjects: LCSH: Cranes, derricks, etc.–Juvenile literature.
Classification: LCC TJ1363 .B794 2017 (print) | LCC TJ1363 (ebook) | DDC 621.8/72–dc23
LC record available at https://lccn.loc.gov/2016033332

Editor: Christina Leighton   Designer: Steve Porter

Printed in the United States of America, North Mankato, MN.

Table of Contents

GOING UP

A crew is building a **skyscraper**. They need a big crane on top of the tower.

First, they use a crane on wheels.

The first crane lifts parts that build the even bigger crane.

Soon, the bigger crane is ready.
Now it can finish the skyscraper!

HEAVY LIFTING

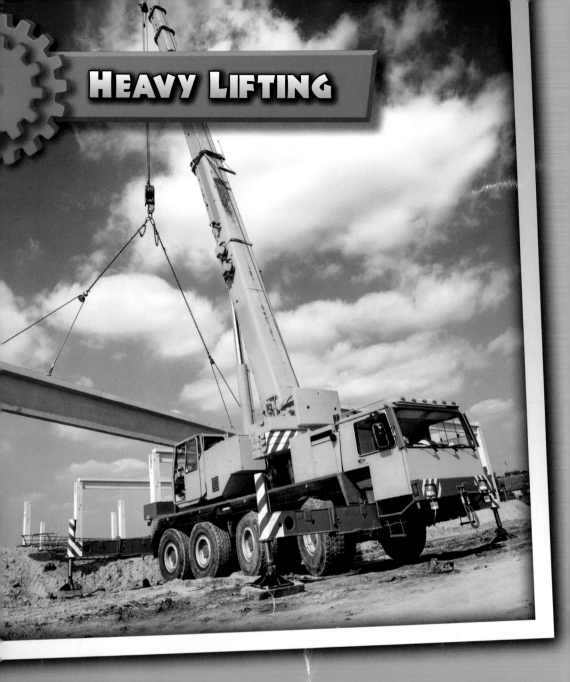

Cranes lift and lower heavy loads.
They come in different sizes.

Tall cranes are often found at **construction sites**. They bring objects to the top of buildings.

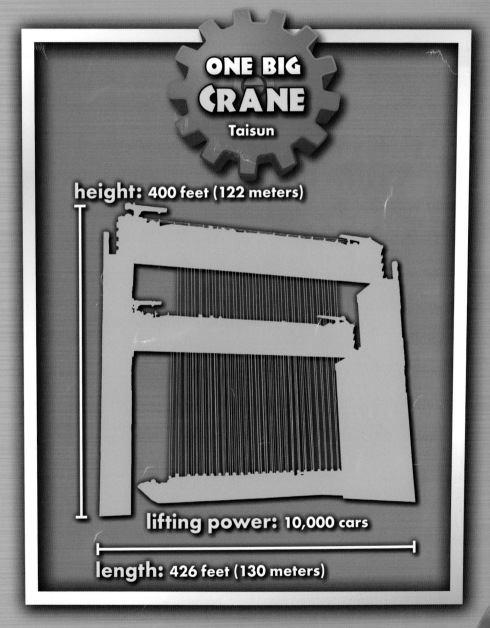

ONE BIG CRANE
Taisun

height: 400 feet (122 meters)

lifting power: 10,000 cars

length: 426 feet (130 meters)

Small cranes work inside factories. They help make machines and parts.

MACHINE PROFILE
GANTRY CRANE

- Moves side to side
- Comes in all sizes
- Works in factories and shipyards

Other cranes are found on water. These build bridges and lift ships or **cargo**.

Some cranes have wheels to move between jobs. Others have **tracks**.

tracks

Cranes are also on helicopters.
They carry loads through the air.

Booms, Jibs, and Cables

Cranes often have a **boom**. This is the crane's long arm.

boom

jib

The boom is connected to the **jib**.
Both parts move to lift the load.

Cables run above the boom and jib. These connect to one or two hooks.

jib

hook

boom

pulley

They form a **lever** and **pulley** system. This makes lifting objects easier.

counterweight

cab

To keep balanced, cranes have
counterweights. These are
usually behind an arm or **cab**.

A worker sits in the cab or uses a radio to control the crane.

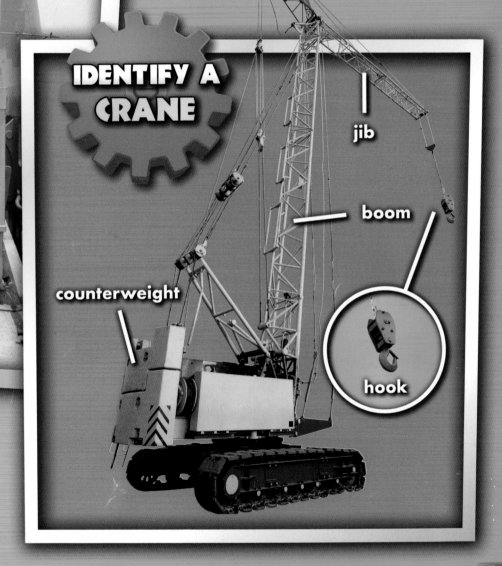

IDENTIFY A CRANE

jib

boom

counterweight

hook

ALL SHAPES AND SIZES

Cranes take many different forms. But they all do similar jobs.

No matter what, they are ready
for heavy lifting!

Glossary

boom—a long arm on a crane

cab—the part of the crane where the driver sits

cargo—something that is carried by a crane

construction sites—places where things are built

counterweights—heavy objects that keep a crane balanced during lifting

jib—an arm of a crane often connected to the boom

lever—a simple machine using bars that makes lifting easier

pulley—a simple machine using ropes and a wheel that makes lifting easier

skyscraper—a tall building with many floors

tracks—large belts that move in a loop around gears

To Learn More

AT THE LIBRARY
Clay, Kathryn. *Cranes.* North Mankato, Minn.:
Capstone Press, 2017.

Hayes, Amy. *Big Cranes.* New York, N.Y.: Cavendish
Square Publishing, 2016.

Osier, Dan. *Cranes.* New York, N.Y.: PowerKids
Press, 2014.

ON THE WEB

Learning more about cranes
is as easy as 1, 2, 3.

1. Go to www.factsurfer.com.

2. Enter "cranes" into the search box.

3. Click the "Surf" button and you will see a
   list of related web sites.

With factsurfer.com, finding more
information is just a click away.

Index

The images in this book are reproduced through the courtesy of: Baloncici, front cover; Anton Gvozdikov, p. 4; ewg3D, pp. 4-5; ollirg, pp. 6-7; Zorandim, p. 8; SasinTipchai, p. 10; Elio Lombardo/ Alamy, pp. 10-11; Kosarev Alexander, p. 12; VanderWolf Images, p. 13; Boris Sosnovyy, p. 14; Wolfgang Grossmann, p. 15; Hellen Sergeyeva, p. 16; Guillermo Velazquez, p. 17; Artit Thongchuea, pp. 18-19; Phant, p. 19; luke james ritchie, pp. 20-21.